This edition first published in 1985 by Dean,
an imprint of The Hamlyn Publishing Group Limited,
Bridge House, 69 London Road, Twickenham,
Middlesex TW1 3SB, England

Text and illustrations
Copyright © The Hamlyn Publishing Group Limited 1981, 1986
Reprinted 1987

ISBN 0 603 00452 0

Printed in Portugal by Resopal

My First Prayer Book

David Christie-Murray
Illustrated by David Barnett

6

Good Morning

Good morning, Jesus.

Thank you for another day. Thank you for all the chances it brings of doing good, of being happy and of making others glad.

Thank you for the joyful sun, smiling down at the earth. Let me not spoil lovely days by being sulky or out of sorts.

Thank you for the clouds and rain that give drink, and bring food to the plants, and make them bring forth flowers and fruit. Let me enjoy wet days because of the good they bring, and not cry because the skies are weeping.

Thank you for wind and snow that make me run to get warm and cause all my blood to tingle. Let me meet and conquer difficulties even if they are harder to run against than the wind, or more horrid than the coldness of wet snow.

Help me so to spend this day that when it ends I shall still be able to say, 'Thank you, Jesus, for today.'

God and Jesus

Dear God,
You are too wonderful for me to know.
You made the sun and moon and all the stars,
　　　more than I can count, and millions more,
　　　too far away for me to see.
You made all animals and birds, noble lions and
　　　gliding tigers, hoppity kangaroos and
　　　toothy crocodiles, funny-voiced ducks
　　　and clucking hens, soaring eagles and tiny
　　　wrens, neighing horses and sad-eyed
　　　cows, tail-wagging dogs and purring cats,
　　　and oh! so many thousands more.

Wherever I look there are insects—spiders and
flies and ants and bees, caterpillars and
butterflies. You made them all.

All around me are trees and bushes, plants and
flowers and blades of grass, as many in a
field as there are stars in the sky. You
made them all and know them every one.

You are too wonderful for me to know.

But you became a baby—like me.

You grew into a child—as I grew.

You grew up to be Jesus, the kindest, most
loving man who has ever lived.

You told everyone, 'God is Love.'

So everything there is has been made by love.

Thank you, God, you who are Jesus, you who
are Love.

People I Don't Like

Dear Jesus,
You told your friends:

> 'Love those who don't like you.
> 'Do good to those who behave
> badly to you.
> 'Pray for those who hurt you or call
> you names.
> 'For then you will be a little more
> like God who is love, for he sends his
> sunshine and rain and all his good things
> equally to those who love him and those
> who don't.'

Dear Jesus,
This is the most difficult thing for any child or
grown-up to do.
Please help me to try.
Help me to get to know all that is good in those I
don't like, as I should like them to know
what is good in me.
Help me always to remember that you love them
as much as you love me, and to see them
as you and those who love them do.
Bring us all one day together as friends, if not on
earth, then happy with you in heaven.
Amen (which means, *'Let it really be
like this.'*)

Pets

Dear Jesus,
Thank you for giving us pets.
Thank you for giving them to us to look after.
Since mine cannot talk to me, help me to
     understand his needs.
Please don't let me forget to feed him and give
     him water and keep him clean.
May I never hurt him, but fondle and stroke him
     and make him feel loved.
In loving him, teach me to grow in love for
     others.
And in being kind to him, help me to learn to be
     kind to everything God has made.
Amen.

Let the Little Children Come to Me

Dear Jesus,
Once, when mothers brought their children to
    you, your friends told them to go away
    and not disturb you.
But you said to your friends:
'Let the little children come to me. Even grown-
    ups who truly want to be my friends must
    come to me with the love and trust that a
    child has for the person he loves best.'
You called the mothers and children back.
You took every child into your arms in turn, and
    cuddled and blessed them all.
If I had been there, you would have cuddled and
    blessed me, too.
I would have snuggled into your strong arms.
I would have felt your kindness wrapped warm
    around me like a cosy rug.
You are alive now and for ever, still loving all the
    children in the world.
Thank you, dear Jesus, for loving me as a child.
    Help me to love you, too, now and
    through all my grown-up life.
                            Goodbye for now.

12

13

Good Friday and Easter

Dear Jesus,
You died on the cross on Good Friday, nearly
      two thousand years ago.
You died in terrible pain of body and still more
      terrible pain of mind, because you took on
      yourself all the dreadful things that have
      happened since the world began, all the
      sadness, all the pain, all the wrong-doing,
      and every death.
A very little of your pain was all the naughty
      things that I have done.
But when you died, they died with you. You
      forgave me.
You did this because you loved me and everyone
      else in the world who has ever lived.
On Easter Sunday you came alive again for ever.
      You talked to your friends. They saw you
      and touched you.
Then you went to prepare a home for them when
      they died and would come alive again
      with you for ever.
And for me, and for all your friends, all down the
      ages, until the end of the world.
Easter time is Spring time, when the world comes
      to life again, as you came to life. The
      leaves are feathery green on the trees.
      There are catkins and pussy-willow and
      sticky buds. Nest-building birds sing all
      day for joy. Lambs and calves and rabbits
      frolic in the fields. Sometimes the days are
      warm with the sun and everyone knows
      that summer is coming.

Thank you, dear Jesus, for dying for me.
Thank you for living again for me.
Thank you for having a home ready for me when
    I die.
Thank you for Good Friday and Easter Day.
Thank you for 'and they all lived happily ever
    after.'

                        Amen.

My Guardian Angel

Dear Jesus,
You once told your friends that every child has an
 angel to look after him, who lives always
 in the very presence of God.
  Please let mine look after me today.
  Let him save me from dangers of
   every kind.
  Let him stop me from doing
   anything naughty or wrong.
  Let him help me to be good and
   kind.
  Let him teach me everything you
   want me to learn.
Please show him how to help me to look after
 myself so that I may become a good and
 wise grown-up.
Thank you, Jesus, for my very own angel.
Goodbye.

My Birthday

Dear Jesus,
    It's my birthday today!
Thank you for bringing me safely through
    another year.
Thank you for all the presents I'll be given and for
    the love of the givers.
Thank you for everything that will make today
    special.

        Let me do nothing to spoil it for
           others.
        Let others do nothing to spoil it for
           me.
        Let me not get too excited and
           tired.
When it's all over, let me not be disappointed and
    fretful and sad.
Tomorrow will be somebody else's birthday.
Let me pray and be happy for them.

Friends

Dear Jesus,
When you lived on earth, you had friends.
Twelve of them loved you so much that they left
	everything and followed you.
Often they did not understand you and you had
	to scold them.
One of them even betrayed you.
You know what it is to have friends who love you
	and yet sometimes hurt you.
Thank you for my friends.
Thank you for my *special* friends.
Let us never quarrel or hurt each other.
But if we do, and it's my fault, make me brave
	enough to say, 'I am sorry.'
If my friend says, 'Sorry,' help me to forgive and
	make friends all over again.
For it is in forgiving and loving each other that
	we deserve to be loved and forgiven by
	you.

			Amen.

Thanks Before a Meal

Thank you, God, for food of so many different
   kinds.

       Tasty things and sweet things,
   meat and vegetables, puddings and
   fruit, foods which give me strength
   and health and help me to
   grow.

Let me never waste food, never be greedy, never
push away what I don't like.
Help me always to remember that others have
such great need that they never get
enough to eat and are always hungry.
When I am grown-up, help me to thank you,
God, for my food, by doing something to
rid the world of hunger.

Amen.

My Five Senses

Dear Jesus,
You have given me five wonderful senses
through which I may know the world.
I see trees and fields and the sky, buildings and
people and streets.
I can paint pictures with exciting colours,
splashing on blues and yellows and
greens and reds.
I can hear voices and sweet music. I can learn to
make music, tunes both merry and sad.
I can smell flowers and hay and scents of every
kind.
I can taste so many different foods, sweet and
savoury, gritty and soft.
I can touch the people and things I love, feeling
smoothness and hardness and glad of
them both.
Thank you, dear Jesus, for all the lovely things
that belong to me through my senses.
Help me to share them with others.
Let me not love them so much that I can never let
them go.
Let me never love things more than people, or
gifts more than givers.
And help me to learn to love you best, the Giver
of all.

Amen.

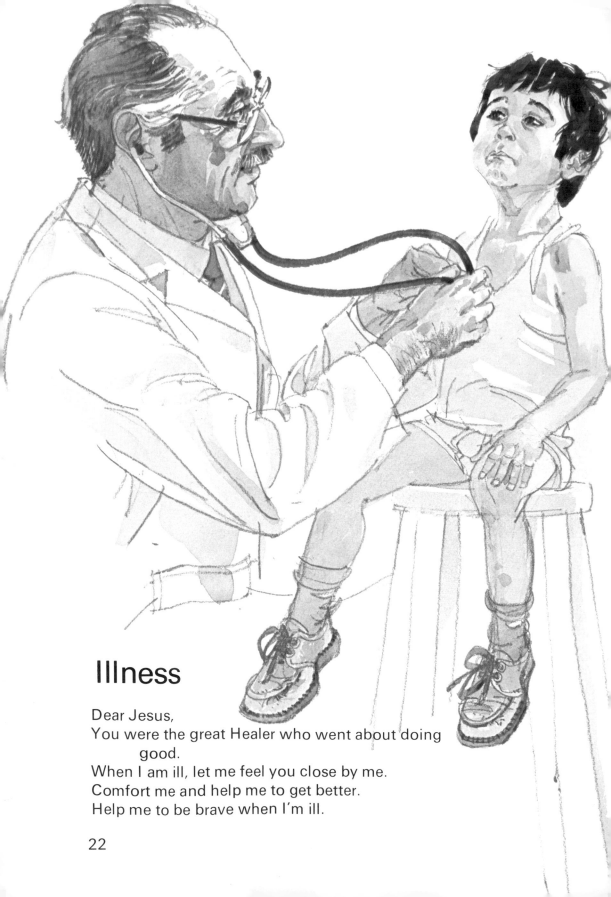

Illness

Dear Jesus,
You were the great Healer who went about doing
    good.
When I am ill, let me feel you close by me.
Comfort me and help me to get better.
Help me to be brave when I'm ill.

22

So many things can go wrong with me.
I can be hurt in so many different ways.

Thank you for doctors and nurses who make me
        well, and for chemists whose medicines
        take away my pain.
Thank you for letting me forget what it's like to
        be ill when I'm well again.
Let me remember then to pray for others who are
        sick and suffering pain, and for all who
        look after them.

Amen.

Fun

Thank you, dear Jesus, for all the fun you give
        me,
For family games and play with my friends,
        for games at school and party games.
Thank you for sometimes letting me be alone.
Thank you for 'Let's pretend' and secret places,
                camps inside bushes, hiding in lofty
                grass, lying below bracken, tree-tall
                against the blue sky, where I talk
                with invisible friends, whom only
                I know.
Thank you for hidey-holes at home, for secrets
        and day-dreams,
                imaginings of lovely kind people to
                play with and beautiful faraway
                sunshiny places to play in.
Let all these help me to live my everyday life,
        and truly to know what's only 'pretend'
        and what's real, and yet to know
        that there is an invisible world that
        is real, where you, dear friend
        Jesus, live, and where I shall one
        day live for ever with you.

Amen.

In the Bath
(For you can talk to God anywhere)

Thank you, God, for bubbles.
Bubbles in my bath with lights in them like
     rainbows.
Soapy bubbles I can blow from a hollow pipe,
     that float and dance like little balloons.
Bubbles of laughter that chuckle like pebbly
     streams.
Bubbles of happiness that sing in me like birds,
     and go "pop" into gladness.
Dear God, give happy bubbles to everyone who
     is sad, and thank you for mine.

24

New Year

Thank you, dear Jesus, for bringing me safely
      to the beginning of another year.
May it be a happy one for my family, for me,
      and for the whole wide world.
  Where there is now hatred, let there
        be love.
  Where there is war, let there be
        peace.
  Where there is sadness, let there be
        joy.
  Where there is hunger, let there be
        food.
  Where people are poor, let them be
        given all they need.
Show me what I must do this year to become
      more truly your friend.
But let me not try to be too good
      and give up when I fail.
Make me brave so that I can go on
      trying right through the year.
Dear Jesus, that is how I can help to make a
      happy year for you.

First Day at School

Dear Jesus,
Today is exciting—my first day at school!
I'm a little frightened because it will all be new.
Make me brave.
Help all other children going to school for the
      first time, some more frightened than I am,
      and give them courage, too.

Thank you for the chance to read and write and
      find out so many wonderful things about
      the world.

Let me never join the others in making a lonely
child more lonely, in keeping him out of
our games, in laughing at him just because
others laugh, in bullying someone weaker
than myself.
Let me understand, too, that sometimes teachers
may be sad or unwell.
Then let me be kind.
So I may be like you who, as you grew up on
earth as a boy, grew also in the love of
God and of all who knew you.

27

Fear of the Dark

Dear Jesus,
Once you were very frightened.
You were in a garden in the dark, left all alone by
      your friends.
You knew that men were coming to catch you
      and take you away to die.
Dear Jesus, I am frightened of the dark. You
      know how I feel because you have been
      frightened, too.
Even though I cannot see you, let me know you
      are there, my friend who will never leave
      me lonely.
You were brave and did not run away.
Teach me to be brave with you, in the dark,
      together.
Goodnight.

Goodnight

For all that has been good today,
      Thank you, Jesus.
For all the things I take for granted that many
      children do not have—enough to eat or
      drink, a home, warmth, clothes and shoes,
      toys to play with, school to teach me,
      people and pets to love and who love me,
      thank you, Jesus.

28

Forgive me if I have been silly or naughty today.
Show me how to forgive others who have been
naughty and nasty to me, so that we can
all be friends again before we sleep, and
wake up happy, to start another day.
Jesus, dear friend, goodnight.